STUNT PERFORMERS

RAY REYES

Rourke
Educational Media

rourkeeducationalmedia.com

Before, During, and After Reading Activities

Before Reading: Building Background Knowledge and Academic Vocabulary

"Before Reading" strategies activate prior knowledge and set a purpose for reading. Before reading a book, it is important to tap into what your child or students already know about the topic. This will help them develop their vocabulary and increase their reading comprehension.

Questions and activities to build background knowledge:
1. *Look at the cover of the book. What will this book be about?*
2. *What do you already know about the topic?*
3. *Let's study the Table of Contents. What will you learn about in the book's chapters?*
4. *What would you like to learn about this topic? Do you think you might learn about it from this book? Why or why not?*

Building Academic Vocabulary

Building academic vocabulary is critical to understanding subject content.
Assist your child or students to gain meaning of the following vocabulary words.

Content Area Vocabulary
Read the list. What do these words mean?

- *adrenaline*
- *elaborate*
- *harness*
- *minimize*
- *perilous*
- *velocity*

During Reading: Writing Component

"During Reading" strategies help to make connections, monitor understanding, generate questions, and stay focused.
1. *While reading, write in your reading journal any questions you have or anything you do not understand.*
2. *After completing each chapter, write a summary of the chapter in your reading journal.*
3. *While reading, make connections with the text and write them in your reading journal.*
   a) *Text to Self – What does this remind me of in my life? What were my feelings when I read this?*
   b) *Text to Text – What does this remind me of in another book I've read? How is this different from other books I've read?*
   c) *Text to World – What does this remind me of in the real world? Have I heard about this before? (News, current events, school, etc....)*

After Reading: Comprehension and Extension Activity

"After Reading" strategies provide an opportunity to summarize, question, reflect, discuss, and respond to text. After reading the book, work on the following questions with your child or students to check their level of reading comprehension and content mastery.
1. *Why do stunt performers risk their lives? (Summarize)*
2. *Why would a stunt performer attempt dangerous motorcycle jumps? (Infer)*
3. *What are some of the dangers that stunt performers face? (Asking questions)*
4. *Have you ever watched a stunt performance in person? Did you wonder what was running through the performer's mind? (Text to Self Connection)*

Extension Activity
Which stunt discussed in the book did you find most interesting? Using books or the internet, research it further. Can you find examples of other record-breaking stunts?

TABLE OF CONTENTS

LICENSE TO
THRILL

Stunt professionals perform **perilous** feats to break records or simply entertain.

 perilous (PER-uhl-uhs): involving great risk or danger

Becoming a Stunt Performer

Stunt performers who work in movies or theme parks train for years. Their work is overseen by special committees.

Action movies involve an army of stunt performers. In every car chase, there are stunt drivers. Fight scenes require martial arts experts.

7

In the *Transformers* movies, stunt performers ran from thousands of gallons of rushing water while boats, cars, and buildings were dropped from the sky.

Stunt woman Janene Carleton was kicked out of skyscrapers and jumped onto moving trucks for the *Mission Impossible* movies.

Special equipment helps stunt performers **minimize** risk on movie sets. Safety wires, airbags, and fireproof clothing are some tools of the trade.

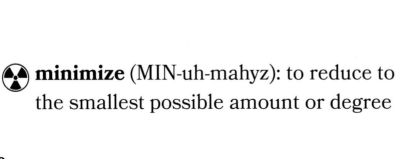 **minimize** (MIN-uh-mahyz): to reduce to the smallest possible amount or degree

A Unique Invention

Stuntman Ken Bates won an Academy Award for Scientific and Technical Achievement after he developed a special wire system for free fall stunts.

Even with safety equipment, accidents happen. In 2009, a stunt performer was paralyzed after a wire **harness** pulled him backward into a wall.

 harness (HAHR-nis): the combination of straps, bands, and other parts forming working gear for people or animals

In 2011, a stunt double suffered a career-ending injury when another performer swung an ax handle and missed the spine protector strapped to his back.

A Fatal Accident

In 2017, professional road racer and stunt driver Joi Harris lost her life on the set of *Deadpool 2*. Joi lost control of the motorcycle she was riding and crashed into a building.

THEY'RE NOT ACTING ANYMORE

Some actors don't use stunt doubles. Action movie star Jackie Chan is famous for starring in **elaborate** martial arts fight scenes.

 elaborate (ih-LAB-er-it): worked out with great care to detail

In the *Mission Impossible* movies, actor Tom Cruise hung from wires outside of the the Burj Khalifa in Dubai, the tallest building in the world.

In another stunt, Tom held the side of a cargo plane as it took off. He wore contact lenses and ear plugs to protect himself against high wind **velocity**.

velocity (vuh-LAH-si-tee): speed

Tragedy Strikes

Brandon Lee was fatally wounded on the set of *The Crow* while performing his own stunt. A fight scene with a gun that fired blanks still had a fragment of a real bullet inside.

MOVERS, SHAKERS, AND RECORD BREAKERS

Some stunt performers don't act in movies. These daredevils perform for the **adrenaline** rush, the roar of the crowd, or to break world records.

☢ **adrenaline** (uh-DREN-el-in): a hormone secreted by the human body in response to stress, anger, or fear

Tightrope walker Nik Wallenda defied gravity on June 15, 2012, when he crossed over Niagara Falls.

Evel Knievel thrilled audiences in the 1970s with his daredevil motorcycle stunts. He once tried to soar over a canyon on a rocket-propelled motorcycle. The jump failed, but his parachute saved him.

American Folk Hero

Evel Knievel had his own
action figures, lunchboxes,
and comic books. He broke
37 bones during his career.

In 2018, 32 stunt performers wore special clothing. Then they were set on fire! They walked around for 45 seconds, setting the Guinness World Record for "Most People Performing Full Body Burns."

Thrill-seeker Anna Cochrane shattered a dizzying record in 2016. She performed a trapeze act while suspended from a hot air balloon 10,365 ft (3,159 m) above New Zealand's coast.

Like Anna Cochrane, this daring artist performs high in the sky.

27

Philippe Petit broke the law to perform a daring stunt. His team used disguises and fake documents to get past security at the World Trade Center towers in 1974. Using a bow and arrow, they launched a wire across the buildings. Philippe then walked across the wire for 45 minutes.

MEMORY GAME

Can you match the image to what you read?

INDEX

SHOW WHAT YOU KNOW

1. Who invented special equipment that slows a performer's free fall without an airbag?

2. How was the world record for "Most People Performing Full Body Burns" set?

3. What did Evel Knievel try to jump over with a rocket-propelled motorcycle?

4. How high in the air did Anna Cochrane go to break the world record trapeze act?

5. Where did Philippe Petit perform his hire-wire act?

FURTHER READING

Besley, Adrian, *YouTube World Records: The World's Greatest Record-Breaking Feats, Stunts and Tricks*, Carlton Books, 2016.

Gerstein, Mordicai, *The Man Who Walked Between the Towers*, Square Fish, 2007.

Guinness World Records 2018: Meet Our Real-Life Superheroes, Guinness World Records, 2017.

ABOUT THE AUTHOR

Ray Reyes is a photographer and former newspaper reporter. He has never performed a stunt, but he has hiked up mountains and dodged giant waves in his travels. In his free time, he enjoys reading, spending time with family and friends, traveling, and binge-watching television shows.

Meet The Author!
www.meetREMauthors.com

www.rourkeeducationalmedia.com

PHOTO CREDITS: Cover, page 1: ©Andy_Oxley; page 5: ©aluxum; page 7: ©Lya_Cattel; page 9: ©ronniechua; page 11: ©tommasolizzul ; page 13: ©Olena Chernenko; page 15: ©tashi_delek; page 17: ©DawidKasza; page 18-19: ©dblight; page 18b: ©Gage Skidmore; page 20: ©davidf; page 24: ©igzz; page 27: ©madsci; page 28: ©mbolina

Edited by: Keli Sipperley
Cover and Interior design by: Rhea Magaro-Wallace

Library of Congress PCN Data

Stunt Performers / Ray Reyes
 (Daring and Dangerous)
 ISBN 978-1-64369-032-2 (hard cover)
 ISBN 978-1-64369-106-0 (soft cover)
 ISBN 978-1-64369-179-4 (e-Book)
Library of Congress Control Number: 2018955850

ɔ 791.43
R330S

3 2872 50154 0888

Rourke Educational Media
Printed in the United States of America,
North Mankato, Minnesota